A Silhouette in Time

Life • Love • Lily

By Lily T. Wu

PACIFIC RAVEN PRESS

Roses whose scents are cherished by all

Water Color, 2020

LTW

© 2021 *A Silhouette in Time: Life, Love, Lily* by Lily T. Wu, Pacific Raven Press, LLC

All rights reserved. This book may not be reproduced, in whole or in part, including illustrations, in any form (beyond that copying permitted by Sections 107 and 108 of the U.S. Copyright Law and except by reviewers for the public press), without written permission from the publisher.

Pacific Raven Press, LLC
Ka'a'awa, Hawai'i 96730

ISBN: 978 0 9993039 3 1

Cover design and concept by Lily T. Wu

Drawings, images, and photographs by Lily T. Wu

Book layout by Eien Design Studio, *www.eiendesignstudio.com*

Executive Editor: Kathryn Takara
Asst. Editor: Isabella T. Le

This work is licensed under Pacific Raven Press, LLC.

Library of Congress Cataloging-in-Publication Data

A Silhouette in Time: Life, Love, Lily by Lily T. Wu
Catalogued as: Poetry, Asian American, Women, Family, Philosophy

Printed in the United States of America

Pacific Raven Press, LLC, is an independent publisher.

http://pacificravenpress.co/
pacificravenpress@yahoo.com

Self-portrait, Pencil drawing 2018

DEDICATION
To the four important men in my life
My Beloved Father, my Two Sons and my Husband
To my Mother and Daughter

Table of Contents

DEDICATION iii
Introduction: ...Arrangement By God ix

Prologue: ...and Happiness We Will Know 1

Pencil Drawing: Hummingbird 3

Of Winters…And of Summers 5

The Naïve is learned 6
Quiet Sound of a Broken Heart 7
Budding Flower 8
Beauty Emerging from Mud 9
Heaven's Recompense 10
Time Had Already Said Good-Bye 11
Time Passed 12
What Life Has Installed? 13
Fallen Dreams 14
Neither Woman Nor Child 15
Life Like the Lawn 16
The Aged Old Shores 17
Perfect Knight 18
White Knight 19
Lovers and the Mist 20
The Dream That Was Once Mine 21
Hands of Duty 22
Dreams Left to Chances 23
Heart and Mind 24
It Will Come, When It Comes 25
Letters Before We Meet 26
Time Capsule 27
Pencil Drawing: Indigo Bunting 28

Of Fire... And of Water 30
Of Fire...And of Water 31
The key to success 32
An Ocean Apart 33
Patiently Waiting... 34
Lighter Melody 35
Floating Above Clouds 36
Warmth of a Smile 37
Once Written, It Became a Part of Me 38
I Want 39
Love...Beyond Him and I 40
Fire and Water 41
...Reality 42
Love Needs Nourishment 43
Reality Seeps In 44
Years Come and Go 45
The Smile 46
Feelings Are in the Mind 47
The Many Roads of Destiny 48
Life's Lessons 49
Each Step, A Journey 50
Ice Slowly Melting 51
Unavoidable Fate 52
Let It 53
Marriage Bound 54
Eat Your Ice Cream Before It Melts! 55
Pencil Drawings, Photo: Carol, Lily, Isabella 58
Of Springs.... And of Falls 59

Of Springs....And of Falls 61
Pencil drawing: New leaves emerge 62

v

Strolling Down the Path of Time 63
Taking a Deep Breath 64
My Home 65
In Mom's Home 66
Luxury of Childhood 67
Happy Eager Face 68
Oh, How Scared I Was! 69
Isabella 70
Alan 71
Andre 72
Bond of Love 73
Portraits of My Parents 75
The Candle that Burned Brightly *(Eulogy for my Father)* 76
Enjoy Each and Every Breath 78
If You Must Say Good-Night 79
If Tomorrow Never Comes 80
The Wind Speaks to the Sun's Rays 81
Why Ask, "Why?" 82
Pause…..Breathe 83
This Time! 84
Along the Shore of Friendship 85
Taking Chances 86
How can we sustain our emotions? 87
To let the light in 88

Of Husband…And of His Wife 89

Breathe easily for the life that is given 90
Shooting Stars 91
Joy, On Love's Golden Wing, *(To my Husband)* 92
We Are Now… One! 93
As a Wife Should 94
It Was All Worth It! 96

My Castle 98
Leaves Upon the Tree 99
My Shelter 100
The Parts and Parcels of Who We Are 101
Arrangement By God 102
Embracing Happiness 103
In the Wee Hours of Our Life 104
Finicky of a Rose's Life 105
Morning Rituals...Sipping Coffee 108
Early Morning and Evening Symphony 111
He said he would give his life for me 113
Heart's Reflection 114
Balance of the Four Seasons 115
The Webs of Our Life 116
Woman in Veil 118
A Silhouette in Time 119
Fool or Wise 120

Epilogue "...In Reaching the Shore" **121**

A Poet's Final Note....The Poetic Mind 123

Acknowledgements 125
About the Author 129

Introduction
Arrangement By God...

One's life is dependent upon the internal force of one's will and the external force that is driven from up above, *Arrangement by God...*

At times the secrets we may want to bury deep within our soul will somehow find a way to surface, be it physical, emotional, or metaphysical. Some of us live in this internal world that we've created for ourselves.

An artist without boundaries may not discipline her craft. A person with too many boundaries will never appreciate the artistic world that can transcend the common place to the ethereal. So, the push and pull of the two worlds-the right and left mind- and the tension created is the ultimate challenge in life.

Being an introvert living amongst extroverts (more than a dozen siblings!), I would also learn to safeguard my feelings and emotions, externally. (Often times, it was too deep of a sacrifice for a young person in those formative years, to handle.) My internal world and thoughts -the place I would run to and give life to-are the making and the basis of my poetry. Thus the good, the bad, and the moments that define our lives in becoming who we are.

Prologue
...and Happiness We Will Know

We are the sum and parts of our experiences, part and parcel of the exchanges with the people we crossed paths with, and the interplay of the internal and external forces that rule our destinies.

To the Frenchman and the *Butterfly Effect* of crossing a path with him for less than a few seconds on the street of Paris. He, whom I do not even know his name nor can recollect what he looks like, but in this life I owe much to him.

While about to finish crossing a busy intersection, with an ice cream parlor on the other side, I was delighted when a young Frenchman stood gallantly waiting with an ice cream cone as a gift to me, perhaps in appreciation of my gentle aura from across the street. As I was taken by surprise, I hadn't stopped my saunter and upon graciously accepting the cone, thanked him with a genuine laugh and continued on my way with my oldest and youngest sisters flanking me. It was a pleasantly sweet moment though no words were exchanged, just smiles of appreciation between the two of us.

The pure joy of youthfulness, beauty and the magical air of romance that Paris has always promised would leave a lasting impression. That brief but delightful encounter would take me through some of the loneliest parts of my life, when I felt anything but beautiful.

Over a quarter century later, I would recall why that moment had been so poignant. It taught me that even in the few seconds of crossing a path with someone, the *Butterfly Effect* of that one moment in time could reverberate throughout the rest of one's life.

However, many of life's exchanges are never singular and isolated; many have cause and effect. In order for the moment to remain beautiful, it needs to be pure. The more exchanges we have with one another, the more complex emotions can become involved. Thus, those singular and pure moments are often needed to offset life's many volatile interchanges.

Just as someone had teased me, called me names, and made me feel as the ugly duckling living amongst swans, that one teasing comment was so detrimental to me in my formative youth, and the ensuing consequences thereafter…

Now, perhaps the happiness is that the duckling did indeed transform into a swan. Those years of quiet introspection and perhaps the early knowledge acquired, revealed that the essence of a true swan is just as important as its physical attributes. When internal and external karmas are aligned, it is the epitome of true beauty, and signifies the profound happiness that I've come to know and have spent my life striving for.

To my husband, his first act as a gentleman on the phone those many years ago was greatly admired and appreciated. Though through life we had our basic guiding elements to conquer, the destructive forces of *Fire and Water*, he remains to be the only man I've truly ever known. He is always in possession of an important key to my happiness.

Hummingbird
Pencil drawing 2010

Symbolizes joy, love and to be present in the moment
She is always in constant pursuit of the sweetness in life
Her long beak will be able to break through to the unpleasant part of the flowers, to get to the sweet nectars

Despite her small size, she is tenacious, independent, and resilient
She has the rare ability to fly backward as she is adaptable
She accepts the reality of change with a happy heart

She also symbolizes continuity and infinity

Of Winters...
And of Summers

The naïve is learned
Pain ages the soul.

Circa 1985

Quiet Sound of a Broken Heart

If you close your eyes and listen
Very carefully
You will be able to hear
The sound of quiet fluttering
Of a bird's wings
As it takes flight
The rustling echoes
Of the aged bamboo
As it hums to you
The trickling water
That comes rolling over
The stepping-stones
To join its sibling's
In the cool lonely pond
Close your eyes, still
And listen awhile longer
When you think you will hear no more
It will come to you
That the sound you hear
Is the crying
Of my broken heart.

Budding Flower

And God has written
Where the seed shall fall
Barely a bud
Yet stripped of its stem.

Lotus and Lily,
Beauty Emerging from Mud

Visions of days past
Visions of days coming
My eyes are written
My hands play no note
My heart's embittered
My mind uncontrolled
And love, like leaves to the wind
Mud still remains
Dirty and bestridden
Up springs new hope
Stem, still deeply buried in soil.

Heaven's Recompense

And the heavens will recompense
For all the tears of yesteryears
The most bountiful dewdrops
Will bring forth a beautiful garden ahead
Patience, patience, my little bud in bloom
Patience, patience, my little bud in bloom.

Time Had Already Said Good-Bye

Time had already said good-bye
To leaves and grasses that had grown dry
And roses whose scents are cherished by all
Hold no true charm for me anymore
Colors that fade as seasons climbed on
No hues can hold back the rule of dawn
Happiness and sorrow, we will know
Alas, sorrow and happiness that make one grow

Spring comes on fighting winter's chill
Life goes on despite what one feels
Coldness of winter had warmth in those arms
Never imagining it could lead to harm
Alas, the blanket had gone leaving me bare
And in time someone came to share
The burden of winter, yet winter's to come
The agony of love, still foreign to some

The wind had blown upon our backs
Sadness is in looking toward the forbidden track
So happy are young lovers who had found love
Always chasing rainbows atop the wings of dove
Why can't I be the one to soar tonight?
Why does my love never turn out right?
I can't foretell what's to happen ahead
Only wishing no thorns lay upon this bed.

Time Passed

Time passed
  Nothing left
    Only memories
      Only regrets

Nothing is permanent
  Only memories
  are what's left
    of yesterdays'
      laughter and tears

No feelings
  Only numbness
    And acceptance
      And forlornness
        And silence

It is finally goodbye
And no more turning back

Why does the heart still ache?
Why does the mist never subside?
Why does the mind still remember?

What Life Has Installed?

I wonder what life has installed for me?
I wonder what I will do?
Who I will meet?
And will I be happy?
I wonder if I will make the right decisions?

Fallen Dreams

Dreams have fallen
To the stream
Pride shattered
From reckless whims
Shadow hides
Hurt dignity
Tears flowing
Silently.

Neither Woman Nor Child

So disillusioned and confused
Between the two persons within
Neither woman, nor child
Wanting both
Yet none.

Life Like the Lawn

Like the grass we've just plugged in our lawn
The weeds keep creeping into every part of the ground
As you pull them out, new ones emerge springing with life
Wanting to take over, and soon they are uncontrollable
But still you have to try.

If the foundation was put properly from the beginning
With one step appropriately put before another
The weeds would have been more in check
Once you made the wrong decision
Or put things in the wrong order
It takes so much more effort
To make things right again
But still you have to try.

The Aged Old Shores

Time passes, yet some beauties still remain the same
Like the waves that rush upon the rocks
And never cease to stop
Like the sounds of water hitting against the aged old shores
Breaking up the stillness of midday
Like the birds soaring and plunging high above
Picking out the seeds from blossoming trees
And like the endless sky above
That never ceases to bring hope
To a lonesome heart at sea.

Perfect Knight

My heart wanders aimlessly in the night
Searching for my perfect knight
It has met so many misfortunes
I have fallen out of my path
My needs are insatiable.

White Knight

The valor of the White Knight
Can only be measured by
The degree of difficulties
In the paths that lay ahead
And the many hurdles
He would be forced to climb.

Lovers and the Mist

Dreams take me away if you will

Take me to places quiet and still

To the cove far out

Beyond the sea

Where seagulls come calling to me

Where soft, ethereal mist blinding everything in sight

Only reveals my lover, beneath the pale moon light

And the world knows no beginning, nor end

Only my lover and me

Until the

End

•

The Dream That Was Once Mine

The dream that was once mine
Is but a mist
Within a mist

Never tangible
Forever floating
Through my craving fingers

I see it
And yet,
It is incomprehensible

It envelops me
And yet,
It can never be mine

Is life but a dream?

Hands of Duty

Where do I stand in time?
Present, past, and a future yet to unfold
Where will I go from here?
I'm destined to be bound
By the hands of duty
No life is left in this heart
Only a flicker of a flame
One blow
And I'll be free.

Dreams Left to Chances

Dreams left to chances

Yielding and forgiving

Time, so unhurried

Neither paths nor obstacles

Consequence

To none.

Heart and Mind

Where my heart fails
My mind will urge me on
Where I am fragile
My mind will force me to be strong
Where I shed tears
My mind will grow with every drop
Where your heart is unwavering
Your mind will not leave you at ease
If your heart and mind are stolid
I will hold onto my soul.

It Will Come, When It Comes

It will come, when it comes
However hard you try
However where you look
However more you think
However hard you fight
It will come, when it comes

How surely you will know
How surely you will glow
How surely your heart skips
Oh...how surely you will know
It will come, when it comes.

Letters Before We Meet

Without meeting too early
We fantasized too much
Letters are only great for a short duration apart

Without mundane things
We fantasized too much
Letters do not replace experiences
In those critical hours of... our knowing...

Time Capsule

Ping-Pong letters of lovers written
To remind our future selves

Tender words we've imprinted
To carry us through whatever may
The future unfolds

Letters stretching from the Great Walls of China,
To the many Island Paradise, Texas, Arkansas,
And along the shores of the Atlantic Coast

Eruditions of who we are
Encapsulating our heart and mind
Retrievable for future withdrawals

These *Ping-Pong* letters
Time capsuled
From You and Me.

Indigo Bunting
Pencil drawing 2009

Symbolizes knowledge, intelligence
Joy and purity

She is often secretive and understated
She can conceal herself amongst the foliage, however
When emotions need to surface, she will sing her beautiful songs

Of Fire... *And of* Water

It is always the respect and appreciation of someone dear to us that will become our focus, our driving force, and ultimate goal in life.

Though a man's motives and ambitions are always of a physical, financial, or tangible focus, be it attainment of properties, titles and securities for himself or his family as a provider. A woman, and especially one so introverted like myself, our focuses are always of a more emotional nature. Emotional experiences and emotional wealth-intangible and incomprehensible- at times even to ourselves, are what we seemingly need to have or acquire in life, whether we rise or fall in its pursuit.

This Collection is dedicated to my husband who has given me the stability needed and the peace of mind to live in comfort so that I may go into my own world. My husband has been a rock; a constant force in my life, oftentimes unwavering in his own path and emotions.

Whereas the soul of a poet who feeds on our emotions and thus our heart, may wane and wander wherever the gentlest of winds take us, at times through stormy weather, through fragrant mists or through pungent emotional paths that we find ourselves caught in.

Without his steadfast nature, perhaps I would have wandered aimlessly in my own forest, without the smallest glimmer of light to guide me home. He is the white pebbles* that I had strewn along this treacherous path of a jungle in life that I follow, always backtracking slowly home.

Without the *Fire and Water* elements in our life, these poems may have never needed to be written. We are thus destined to be whom we are with in this life as foretold by the *Shooting Stars*.

* In reference to *Hansel and Gretel*

Of Fire...
And of Water

The key to success
Is to keep your eyes where they should be
In front of you.

Photo Credit: Hoang, Circa 2001

An Ocean Apart

I'm not really sure what has come over me
Daydreaming night and day
Can't seem to get my mind off of you
I'm not even sure if I want to
Time is precious and running short
My test is tomorrow, but still...
I can't concentrate on studies

One thing keeps floating in my mind
How I yearn to see you, to be with you
For, how little I know you
What I've been fighting inside
Has but finally surfaced at last
For once a drop of water leaks
Nothing will stop it from streaming wild
Hopefully, it will reach your shore someday.

Patiently Waiting…

Sitting here…working…
Remembering…
Feeling…hurting…
How much longer will it be…

I'm counting
The years…the months
The weeks…"*The Day*"
The hours…the minutes…
Our heart beats…
My weakness…

Across our adopted land you lay
Sleeping…thinking…
I miss…your presence…
Your warmth…your arms…
Our silence

Nothing matters…only
Your love…your guidance.

Lighter Melody

Lying in the shadow of darkness
Songs streaming softly to my ears
Beautiful songs of endearment
How I yearn to be with you
Sharing each word, each melody
Under a moonless summer night
Where are the stars tonight?
So dim before my eyes
The laughter has all gone
Only the stillness of the night by my side
No breeze to hurry me onward
Sympathetic to my aching heart
Waiting patiently for the stars to glisten
And a lighter melody to hum along.

Floating Above Clouds

Lying in the shadow of darkness
Can't seem to fall asleep
Images of you keep floating in my mind
Tearing away at my heart
My sister's words suddenly remind me
How very true it all seems now
"...Never fall in love when you're still young...
It will be very hard to concentrate on school..."
Nothing else can take my mind away
Even if tomorrow's test could mean failure!

Suddenly everything seems so ironic
I recall telling a friend
How strong my heart is, how icy it is
Now I'm weaker than a feather
Can't seem to get my feet on the ground

Floating above clouds beyond reach
And time is but centuries away...
You did not want to disturb me at first
But instead, you disturbed my heart
And I thought I was so strong
But now ...I can't fight this feeling any longer...

Warmth of a Smile

If I love you, then forgive me
For I cannot help but love the person
Whose warm smile melts away the sadness
Of my agonizing heart
Whose understanding eyes
Releases the doubt
Of my troubled world
Whose untouchable heart
I cannot but win.

Once Written, It Became a Part of Me

Trying to recall all the poems
I've written and thrown away
It is hard to remember those lines that
Revealed so much of me

What is gone can be no more
Is that true of life, I wonder…

No, it's just hidden within me
For once written, it became a part of me
Like the people I've met and the things long past
They're asleep in me somewhere

Burning papers won't suppress
What part of life I'm longing to forget

Hoping the poems that still remain
And the life that is still ahead
Will not be wasted in the
Sorrowful search of my past.

I Want

I want your world to be mine

Happiness or sorrow to be shared

Let me mend your wings

Let us guide each other

Tomorrow means nothing without you.

Love...Beyond Him and I

I will never stop caring
For those who have shared
Part of their lives with me
But caring only in soul
And always hoping
For the best that life can bring them

For now my thoughts
And feelings belong to a special person
Whom I shall love, respect, and always
Be faithful to

My heart will always belong to his
In a very special way, and yet
There are many ways to care for people
My love is his completely, and yet
There is room enough to care for the whole world
Beyond him and I.

Fire and Water

Fire and water
Always at odds
Always repelling

Fire and water
Always hot
Always simmering

Fire and water
Always attracting
Always demanding

Fire and water
Always smoldering
Always fuming

Fire and water
Always ebbing
Always receding.

…Reality

The daydreaming has gone from my eyes
All that's left is ………R E A L I T Y !
Love exists only in words
Love to be accepted
I wish….

Love Needs Nourishment

The beauty of love is
It's impermanence
If not nurtured
It will
Die
!

Reality Seeps In

The dream has gone
And reality seeps in
Cannot life be but a dream?
Is reality so unkind?

Waking up cold and empty
Once warm by a glimmer of hope
Of reaching out to one
Who was so understanding

How forlorn life really is
To be without a companion
To share special dreams
And special moments
With one who is closest to the heart.

Years Come and Go

The years come and go, as they often do
With no need of permission or appointment
From who knows, whom?

At times it creeps up, but mostly it passes by
With no apology as to why
For some the years have been more than kind

For others still longing to fight back
The hands of time
With their hopes and frustrations, pushing them on

Yet, linger awhile longer
And the pain
Will surely come.

The Smile

The smile is captured in my memories
As well as…….your…… soft glances
But alas, we are still strangers
Sharing only a smile
And a glance

●

Feelings Are in the Mind

Why?
What purpose does it serve to meet
A person you like
Would like to know better
If only for an hour
To satisfy that hunger
In your mind
And feelings are all
In the mind
For that one glance, one smile
And making it last forever
In your mind.

The Many Roads of Destiny

The many roads of destiny
Here we stand at an impasse
The temptress and tempter abound
To see what weaknesses abate

The morn will tell its true tale told
To those that thus listen with
The roads of the heart
Of the soul
Of the mind

The burden of consciences
And the faithfulness of responsibilities

To all who must ride in the aftermath
Of the eventful storm
Of life.

Life's Lessons

All lessons are called upon
In time of import
Life's lessons
Crucial test abate

In earnest
He who learned
Shall pass

He who wavered
Shall falter

To repeat
Once again
Life's trodden path

Till the lessons are ingrained
Into the consciousness
Till the path is cleared
For the victor.

Each Step, A Journey

All thoughts come crisscrossed in my mind
How to get back to the day before it all began
A child, a young wanderer
A woman, confidences abound

Each step, a journey
Each mishap, a lesson

Painful as they may be
Have cloaked and sheltered me
From the imminent danger of "Being".

Ice Slowly Melting

The thawing process has started
As air entering the divine body
Feelings shelved long ago
In the forgotten arctic
Ice slowly melting
Ice slowly melting

Success is a lonesome entity
Heartbeats are driven by complex forces
Anger, pain, humiliation and atonement
The rotating wheel of emotions

A focus to resilience
To conquer all, to become all
An anomaly in the desert
Ice slowly melting
Ice slowly melting

It's intrinsic property
Slowly
Revealing.

Unavoidable Fate

In the midst of the madness
Strength is born to conquer the soul
Weakened by unavoidable fate
That must now be faced to eradicate
The marks that were made long ago

And the pain that was suppressed for even longer

That unavoidable fate, which now must be faced
To give strength to the soul
And find the peace that must surface
To pave way for life's beauty
That was hidden amongst the mist

Forgiveness, was the key

To unlock the breadths within the soul
To give breeze to the mist
And clear the path for sunshine
That has been there, waiting all along.

Let It

Let the mind wander

Let it slip-slide in vignettes

Let it visit old times and cherished memories

Let it glide through the tunnel of emotions

Let it revisit the cause and effect of things

Let it draw strength from the past—whatever it may be

And whatever it will be

Let it have a place in the heart

Let it make its peace internally.

Marriage Bound

The winding and gnarled path has lead us
To this place of haven we call home
My friend and lover who has stood beside me
In this treacherous path of marriage-bound
Patiently waiting for the heart and mind to heal.

Eat Your Ice Cream Before It Melts!

Perhaps with Coronavirus still fresh in our mind
And the uncertainty of the future
Now universally felt by most everyone
Perhaps it is time now and not to wait
To eat your ice cream before it's a little too late…

Do not wait to tell her you love her
As you look deeply into her eyes
Do not wait to compliment her on her cooking
As you partake those dishes and savor those sweet pies
Do not take her for granted
As in everything in life, all partying must come to an end

Do tell her she is beautiful
A husband's compliment trumps all
Don't wait till the thought that you may lose her
To know that you can never live without her

Do not wait to kiss her smooth face
And caress her slender curves
Love her most indefinitely, and love her without reserve
For time does not wait for anyone
And time is the enemy of all women

Do not wait to appreciate and hold her dearly in a warm embrace
Give her flowers, praises, and make sweet memories
With laughter in all the many different places
For comes a day, somewhere in the future
The inevitability of a lover's parting will come

Thus, I bid you dearly, do not wait
To enjoy the ice cream cone with her now
Before it is too late
Eat your ice cream before it melts!

Pencil Drawings:

Carol, my Mom 1998
Lily circa 1985
Isabella, my Daughter 2019

Of Springs…..

This chapter is especially dedicated to my three beautiful and wonderful children. They are like the air that I breathe in each day. In raising them, I have found the ultimate happiness of being a woman. Their needs for me as children gave me the strength that was necessary, when perhaps certain of my dreams had fallen apart. They are the joy of a woman who has so much love to give and who was also in need to feel appreciated and cherished at the same time.

And of Falls

To my beautiful mom Carol and the unimaginable strength of a woman! In my defense of her when asked how many children she had, *"Thirteen!"* Most would reply, *"The poor woman…. "* I would then exclaim, *"She was well-loved"* by her husband, and he in return was *"well-loved"* by her.

Perhaps the most important person in my life remains to be my father, Michael. His love and integrity are the guiding principles in my life, even long after his demise. He has remained to be my idol. His early lessons to empower oneself with knowledge, the internal forces within you which can never be taken away, even by the external forces of life, which may never be within the realm of your control anyway.

I would learn the darkness and lightness of life early on. I saw my father, the once all too powerful businessman, upon leaving his country, give up everything in order to safeguard his huge family and secure our freedom. In a blink of an eye, he had lost everything that he had worked so hard for, and which had taken him many years to build. I learned nothing could ever be guaranteed in life.

I would also learn the importance of endurance, sacrifice, and pride in the hard work it would take to start all over again. The resilience of mind needed to rise, fall, and rise again, and that the responsibilities at times rested on that heavily burdened shoulder.

As a young child, I had asked God if he needed to sacrifice anyone in our family, to take... ME! as there were many of us, and to protect my dear Father! because he was the guiding light that all of us depended upon.

When endowed with my own children...I knew I would fight tooth and nail for my right to be here. The need to welcome and tend to *Springs and Summers,* as we leave the *Falls and Winters* of our life behind.

Upon his passing, I have lived my life to uphold the honor and sacrifices that he had given to all of his children. He would be extremely proud now to know that his daughter is greatly respected and admired by many, including high caliber professionals.

Of Springs...
And of Falls

New leaves emerge
As the aged leaves fall
Life has room, but for a moment of intersection
Between births…and the emergence of rebirths.

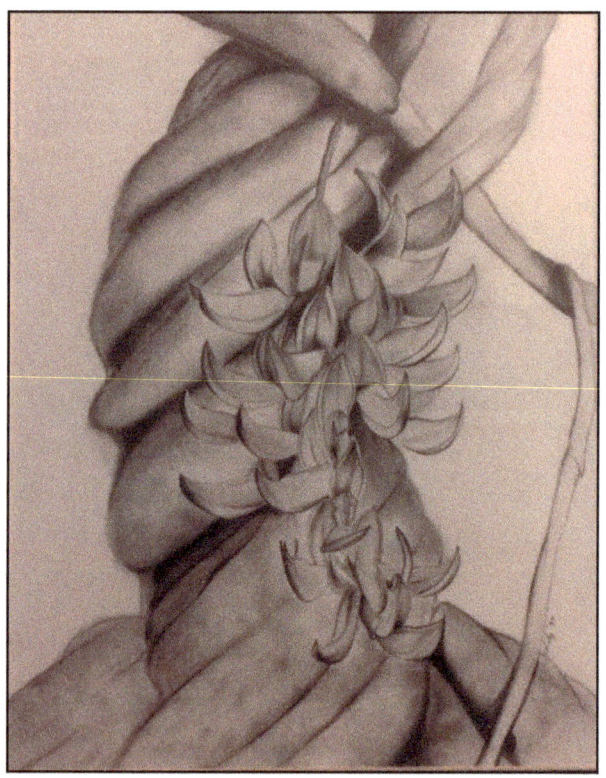

Pencil Drawing 1999

Strolling Down the Path of Time

Strolling down the path of time
I smile on all that has happened
The moments worth remembering
Are those spent in my childhood
So carefree, so happy

Times spent
With brothers and sisters
Times spent
With my Mom, Dad
And others

Stepping out into reality
I smile on all that may happen
The songs yet to be sung
The good-byes for a joyful stride
Down to another place and time.

Taking a Deep Breath

Sometimes when things get to be too much for me to handle
I reach back to the simplest things in life
Like taking a deep breath
And remembering my childhood
Of all the fun I used to have
Like remembering the days' past
When I sat on my Daddy's lap
And stole a whisker from his chin

Like remembering my own adolescence
And how I used to be so innocent
Of the where and how babies came to be
And of my own sensuality
Sometimes these things help me put things in perspective
And help me to become more receptive
To the sorrows, the hardships, and the pains
Of the world all around me.

My Home

Pink, orange and fuchsia colored bougainvillea brighten up the day
Red hibiscus and fragrant tiare flowers, captive against
    their green foliage
Vivid blue colors of the pool, the ocean, the skies
All makes a candy treat for the eyes
The ever-changing view of the bay
The calmness of the neighborhood
Everything makes for a pleasant stay

Birds chirping in the morn
Butterflies fluttering on occasion
Shadow of the leaves, playing behind the drapes, when the
    sunlight dances upon it
Sweet smell of the orange blossoms, and the
    soft breeze that gently sways
Upon the curtain of the autograph trees, standing prominently by
Everything makes for a pleasant stay.

In Mom's Home

The quietness of summer
The calmness of day
Breezes gently swaying the palm leaves
Birds chirping sweetly in Mom's garden

An oasis for the wearied soul
A comfort to come home
Laying snuggled in a familiar bed
Drifting, meandering through yesteryears
In Mom's home.

Luxury of Childhood

I've walked this way a thousand times before
My heart commands me to turn
I obey obediently, as always
Without pause, without concern

A lonesome silhouette against the dawning sky
Looking up, I soak in all that surrounds me
The air feels especially fresh today--strange
Perhaps a part of the burden unloaded itself today
Life is life after all-no mystery to unravel
No more mountains to climb

I remember that scent so well
Soft rain falling--ah yes, I remember
Days of endless rest--summer with no end in sight
Lazy mornings bringing on cool afternoons
Atop a simple bed, with a light blanket
And a novel to cuddle me through the days

The luxuries of childhood that are easily forgotten
Now, with my child in arms
The luxury is once again reacquainted
Without guilt, without concern.

Happy Eager Face

Remembering the time you were on the bed
As you saw me your eyes lit up
And you crawled as fast as you could to come to me
I, on the other hand, tried to run as fast as I could
To try to stop you from falling off the bed

You were so happy you jumped up to greet me
But too late, I did not reach you in time
You fell and cried, I consoled you
But could not erase that happy eager face
So young...so innocent...so brave...yet so disappointed
When you fell

Though the pain was only temporary
For, although I tried to prevent the same situation
From happening again
I knew that no matter where you go, you will find
Something to climb onto, jump off of
Or just get caught in

In a way that makes me glad, because I do
Want you to climb as high as you can
To explore your potentials, with that same eager face

But I also want to be there to catch you
Or be able to comfort you, if things should get a little
Too much for your tender heart to handle.

Oh, How Scared I Was!

Remembering a time when you were sick
Oh, how scared I was!
Your little body seemed to tremble so
Oh, how scared I was!
Your fevered, small body...your tears
Oh, how scared I was!
Putting you into a bucket full of ice
Oh, how scared I was!
To try to bring the temperature down
Oh, how scared I was!
Your flesh against the cold water...your crying!
Oh, how scared I was!
I wish I could take all the sickness from you
I wish I could have all your ear infections, all
Your mumps and measles and
Whatever else the world has installed for you
Oh, how scared I was!

Isabella

Remembering the first moment I saw you
Oh how peaceful my heart was
All the pain seemed to vanish, and
Agony was worth my prize

Your wide eyes, your beautiful smile…
Your small hands and feet
Everything seems so beautiful
All because I love you so
All because you belong to me

I never knew such powerful feelings
Such warmth and enduring peace
Could come from this small bundle

You came into my world, depending on me for life
Yet, without knowing, you've given life's reason
Back to me…Isabella …I love you.

Alan

Alan, my sweet sweet son
I never knew how I would feel with a boy
I thought I couldn't understand you as well
But oh, how I came to love you instantly, and
Oh, but what a boy you proved to be

The rare moments that I held you in my arms
With your face next to my bosom
Oh how happy I felt, like a true mother with her babe

Other times you seemed to be
Fighting, screaming and crying in my arms
Never sitting still for a moment
Never letting me rock you to sleep
Oh, what a boy you proved to be.

Alan, I love you, my son.

Andre

Wide beautiful eyes mesmerized me to look down
As you lay cradled in my arms
Suckling merrily at my nipples for your instant gratification
Teasing you, I called your name in a whisper
And there it goes, lips transformed to a smile
As eyes gently looked up in knowing fondness

Securely and lovingly I held you even tighter
Pondering what heaven's blessing I'm privy to
Eyes-to-eyes, fingers-to-fingers, mouth-to-nipple
Our daily routine, like in an enchanted dream
Curiously you look up thinking who is this lady
That holds me dearly and possessively

Soon you will be able to give her a name
"Mama" perhaps, "Mommy", and hopefully not too soon…."MOM"
As suckling becomes biting, and as
Holding becomes wrestling
Our days together are filled with adventurous avenues

At times the quietness of your slumber
Is the eye of the friendly storm that is needed
For me to appreciate your true beauty… Andre, I love you.

Bond of Love

Holding you in my arms
Looking into those wide eyes
Seeing you so small
I knew I wanted to protect you
Just then, I wanted the world to be at peace
Wanting nothing to harm my little bundle
I wanted so much
Because, I felt so much
So wonderfully and enormously…Happy!

I wanted so much to hold you always in my arms
Like the way I carried you in that first year
But you grew only too fast
And I couldn't hold you like I did before
But with each passing day
You gave me more and more reasons to love you

Sometimes I get so tired, so tired and exhausted
Sometimes you try my patience
Sometimes I spank and yell at you
But I hope that you know
I will always love you

And that, a mother that I may be

 I, like you, am in the process of learning

A process of finding, and a process of growing

I hope this bond of love between us

Mother and child...will grow stronger and stronger

As years go by

For a growth, stemming from love

Cannot be but otherwise.

Portraits of My Parents

Through all the turmoil and fighting, you've sheltered us
Through all the hardship and suffering, you've nurtured us
Through all the mistakes and pain, you've forgiven us
Through all the laughter and growing…you were there beside us

Your strength and love had but one focus
Your chiding and teaching had but one purpose
Your generosity and humanity had enlightened us
Your integrity and values had guided us

Through your eyes, we've learned the meaning of compassion
Through your heart, we've learned the meaning of charity
Through your words, we've learned the meaning of responsibility
Through you…we've learned to love and appreciate our own families

Thank you for not letting the world rob us of our youth
Thank you for providing us with the best of material goods
Thank you for nourishing us with rich and thoughtful truths
Above all…thank you both for just being the wonderful…YOU!

The Candle that Burned Brightly *(Eulogy for my Father)*

The candle that burned brightly, proudly,
   burns no more
The candle that stretched its reach between two continents,
   stretches no more
The candle that led the way for many, many candles,
   leads no more
The candle that provided warmth and nourishment for years,
   provides no more
The candle that had been our guide, our one certainty
   in this uncertain of world, guides no more

It was not the uncompromising wind that blew out its light
Nor the incessant waves of life that determined its end
Nor the never-ending duties that burned out its spirit
But simply, and regretfully, it was the end of its wick
   that heeded its calling

Take heart oh bright candle
For though thou art not here physically

That candle still burns brightly in the depths of our souls
The echo of your voice still resounds softly in our minds
The image of your face and spirit will never be forgotten
And the lessons of love, of life-your eternal gift-are forever
   ingrained in our hearts

Life, whether long or short must come to an end
Remember its strength, the all-consuming light to still lead us on
Live life with compassion and that candle will never cease to burn
Live life with compassion and that candle will never cease to burn.

Enjoy Each and Every Breath

Only God knows how many breaths are allowed for each of us
So enjoy each and every air we allow into our cavity
Make it as fragrant as possible
Fill it with only things we love
For our cavern is limited
Fill it with only people we love
For our cavern is limited
Fill it with memories of sweetness
Fill it with tenderness and kindness
Fill it with sunshine and rainbows
Fill it with laughter and even tears
For love is sweet and yet bitter
For our cavern is limited
Fill it with only things that are dear to us
For our cavern is limited
Fill it with all that is given to us
Make it as lasting as possible
So enjoy each and every moment we may have
For only God knows how many breaths are allowed for each of us
And only love is everlasting and infinite
Only love is lasting and infinite
And only God knows how many breaths are allowed for each of us.

If You Must Say Good-Night

If you must say goodnight, if only too soon
Then I bid you goodnight, if you must go
I thank God for all the days that you were awake
Keeping me companion, keeping me afloat in this large world

I thank God for all the days that you were a friend
Giving me rides to school, sharing a few laughs along that road
I thank God for all the days, for your gentleness
The lightness of purpose in your presence
Making the day a little brighter for someone that was lost
In the jungle of emotions, a trademark for all "lost" students

I bid you gentleness in your leaving
I bid you lightness in heart as you leave
Knowing I will promise to be a friend, as you once were
To your beautiful life, to your beautiful wife
And to your prosperity, if ever in need

I bid you farewell in your departure
Knowing you were once cherished
And never will be forgotten
I bid you goodnight, if only too soon
If you must go, I bid you goodnight.

If Tomorrow Never Comes

How does one feel knowing that tomorrow will never come?
What does one think, as the last thoughts of consciousness?
What would one do, thinking of the changes that should've been made?
What does one appreciate, as those last breaths are drawn?

Which is harder? The stay'er or the leave'r
Which is harder? Fight the pain or let the pain subside
Which is harder? Going forward, or looking backward to what if's
Which is harder? Breathing or dying

How do you comfort the ones who are left to live?
How do you go on tomorrow, when today you can barely survive?
How do you know if letting go is the only way?
What would you do if that person were the closest to you?

How do you feel knowing that tomorrow will never come?

The Wind Speaks to the Sun's Rays

The wind speaks to the sun's rays
We each have a purpose on this great earth
All are necessary creatures, small and large
Some to shine and bring warmth to humankind
Some to give lightness and cushion others that fall behind
Some stand alone, rising above the clouds for all to wonder
Some blend in with the crowd, and give strength in their numbers

We are all different, yet necessary to humankind
Some come together, so that the few may shine
Some ride the wave, and others are left to stand behind
The water falls and rises depending on the seasons
The tide recedes, only to rise again in full anticipation
Some flowers are enjoyed barely for a day
While others bloom once, to be enjoyed for an entire season

We each have a purpose on this great earth
All are necessary creatures, small and large.

Why Ask, "Why?"

When destiny calls your name
Stand up to accept the inevitable course
Move along with the swells
Dip if you must
And rise again with the effortless waves

The night must come to give you shelter from the blazing sun
The sun must shine, to warm the chill from your core
Night and Day, they must all come
So why ask, "Why?" When such is the evolution of life
Why ask, "Why?"

Pause…..Breathe

Life's humbling and vulnerable moments
Emotionally, physically, and psychologically
Are but a pause button
For you to breathe and readjust your compass
A breather to re-evaluate
What is important in your life
A warning to not take things for granted
As nothing is permanent
Nothing is guaranteed!!!

This Time!

Despite the warnings, we dive right in
Thinking we'll tempt fate
This time!
Perhaps some will conquer
Where others have failed
This time!
What is life, if we all follow?
Rules are meant to be broken
This time!
Perhaps I will win
And show them
This time!
Perhaps I will lose
And show them
This time!

And if not
Next time!

Along the Shore of Friendship

Cool, salty ocean water splashing upon our flowing skirts
The gritty feelings of sand beneath our soles
The warmth of the afternoon sun, kissing our bare shoulders
Feelings of release as we unburden our secrets
A connection one feels, strolling along in parallel paths
Inhaling the blueness of the azure sky and the ocean's mist
Talking, breathing, sharing and pausing to reflect
Upon sacred whispers of the wind and the ocean's rhythms
The burden of a woman's heart, heavy with pride
As only a heart of another woman can empathize
Afternoon walks along the shore of friendship.

Taking Chances

An artist takes a chance
   And draws her dream on canvas
A poet takes a chance
   And shares her soul on paper
A woman takes her chance
   And reveals her "wishes" to the man
A dreamer takes a chance
   As she share her talents with the world.

How can we sustain our emotions?
When life is meaningless without them.

Photo Credit: Tracy Linh, Circa 2019

To let the light in
One must first open the window.

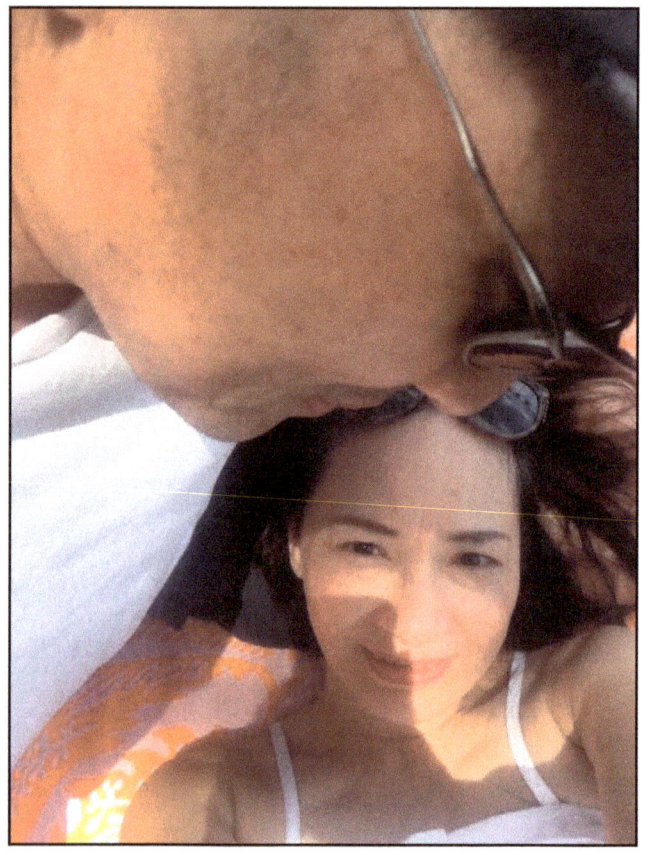

Of Husband...
And of His Wife

Breathe easily for the life that is given
Smile easily for what is given in life.

Shooting Stars

Two seconds

An umbrella

A shooting star

And our destinies are thus determined.

Three children

Another shooting star

The catalyst

And now our souls are interwoven!

Joy, On Love's Golden Wings
To my Husband

Just as I had known sadness
I would have thus now know, **Joy**

Without the indescribable
Melancholy of pining
How could I thus describe, **Joy?**

Without the physical aching heart
Lying in wait for a lover's approach
How shall I now accept, **Joy?**

Without the emptiness
Of an unfulfilled promise
How could I have shown, **Joy?**

Without treasuring the essence of true presence?
Physical proximity aside
How shall I now embrace, **Joy?**

Without rhapsody's magical aura
Satiated by his wanting looks
How could I have never known, **Joy?**

Acclimating cautiously to fill his sphere
I would thus now know ...**Joy!**

We Are Now… One!

I was always glad throughout the years
Though I could never say it out loud
The intimacies and trust between a husband and wife
Are not easily shared with just anyone
There was always the tenderness that I wanted to give
But you were not familiar with my gestures
I wanted to sink myself into you
Digging in deep with my nails
But you had mistaken that need
For hurting you and I could not explain
The desire to dig deeper and deeper into you…

Whatever steps that were taken
To get us both to this point
It is worth all the pain and all the sacrifice
To finally be able to feel the tenderness
Of Husband, and of His Wife
Becoming as one
For as you say
We've won
Because, we are now… One!

As a Wife Should

I had always stood tall
Though feelings may have flowed
As any feelings should
And fought off desire, and fought off needs
To face him squarely
As a wife should

He does not know that I always had his back
When confronted by desire
I had always said no
And told them that I love him
As a wife should

Though I would be in pain
And dreamt of more
But there was always that wall
That no other man could cross
When I knew of the strength that I possessed

I am always in control
Until strength holds me no more
As anyone would buckle, when feelings overflowed
My mind would betray me
The sacrifice for my emotional containment
I am only human
And that is my fragility

He does not know

That it was always for myself

As well as for him

That I was able to stand tall

As a strong woman would

And, as a wife should.

It Was All Worth It!

To see the softness in his eyes
To see the tenderness that he possesses
To see the closeness that we are sharing
To see him happy
It is all worth it

It would take decades of waiting
It would take decades of hurting
It would take decades of tears
But to see us now happy
It is all worth it

To let him in
The risk was great
Opening up to him
After decades of barriers
After decades of suppressions
But to see us together now
It is all worth it

We've lived together
For so long, without being together
We held our own vulnerabilities
And locked them in a safe
We've built castles together
And spared each other's pain

We chose to hold it in
Though we did not see it clearly
That to become one
We needed to not only share our happiness
But our pains and vulnerabilities as well

It would take decades of composure
It would take decades of sacrifice
It would take decades of yearning
But we are finally one
So it was all worth it in the end.

My Castle

He had built me my castles
Along the pristine shores
And we acquired a magical oasis
With koi*, lilies, and lotus galore

He had build me that dream home
But did not ask for what I dreamt
Little did he know
That in his eyes my paradise lay
In his touch my spirits would then fly...

For his gallant effort in saving a bruised swan
He has earned a phoenix's love and devotion
As she rises to spread her wings

He has earned her love
As she hovers over her castle
He has earned her loyalty
As she hovers lovingly... over him.

*Koi - a decorative species of carp kept mainly in water gardens and ponds. Kois are prized for their unique vibrant colors and markings.

Leaves Upon the Tree

We are like the leaves upon the tree
Nothing can hold back the hands of time
We live and we will wither
The elements can be friend or foe
Capture this present moment in time
Love to all that beholds us.

My Shelter

However turbulent the wind comes
He will bestill it
Standing protectively against
The resounding storms
Sheltering and deflecting
Drenching rain and echoing thunder

Winds, whispering change in its passages
Standing endlessly awaiting
Patiently for the storm of life
To never reach my shore
He will bestill it
My Center. My Shelter
My Husband.

The Parts and Parcels of Who We Are

Love, the parts and parcels of who we are
What we have become, and what we have accomplished
And for all the sacrifices that we have made in getting there

Love, for all the right paths, the right decisions
    we were able to make
Along with all the detours, the obstacles, and the
    catalysts along the way
Love, not only of our composed, serene and shiny smiles
Hidden beneath the internal turmoil of tears and fears

Love, not the bits and pieces that shine so brightly
And the many perfect facets we put forth in life
Love, more importantly the under-side of our vulnerabilities
That we were forced to shield, overcome, and left behind

Love, the strength and fire that burns within our heart
For our tears are only revealed to the very selected few
Love, for the parts and parcels of who we are.

Arrangement By God

Patience
Little by little
God will reveal
Our purpose
Here
On this earth
His
Arrangement
In His own
Time.

Embracing Happiness

Further
Distancing
Yourself
From the unpleasantness
Bringing
Happiness
Closer
Surround yourself
With the tranquility.

In the Wee Hours of Our Life

Our life's destinies are foretold in the wee hours of our birth
Looking forward, is like looking backward
Where we are headed, is interlinked with where we came from
Successes and failures are not un-similar
Perhaps it is predestined in the webs of our life
And by the people we have chanced by...

The strength of will,
    will ultimately depend on
The strength of the pain that we have had to endure
To succeed means that we have failed before

The world is a complex wheel in motion
The mind in all of its complexities
Has hidden agendas
Images in our subconscious world
Will find ways to manifest
Bringing desires into the light

In our final moments we will know
Looking backward, we then will be able to step forward
Life and death are not so un-welcoming
This, in the wee hours of our life.

Finicky of a Rose's Life

Lavender, roses, lotus, and soft pink vinca in bloom
A sycophant to my feminine and romantic spirits
Planted, nurtured, cultivated, and prayed
These seeds of hope of a beautiful life
To help me through my most darkest of days

Now it greets me, and I've learned to pause
And give it thanks each morning
I've also learned to plant fragrant lavender roses
The intoxicating smell when they are in bloom
Picking it early and drying it on top of my succulents
To preserve its fragrance for days to come

Its smell still lingers when plucked early enough
Preserving part of its beauty and the short pleasures it gives
Had I waited for the rose to die naturally on its cane
I would have lost its essence's aroma
Such is the finicky of a rose's life
The balance of earth, sky, sun, and water
To produce such beauty
I am willing to wait

Each day I search for new buds in bloom
Each day I wait patiently

The mini rose variety gives me so much pleasure

There's almost for certain a bloom each day
Life's little pleasures, easy to acquire
While I wait for the true rose to bud
Those larger variety blooms once
As it requires more energy, and a long lapse
Before the next blossoming cycle appears again

…As if suctioning in a larger breath of air
Upon knowing the dive is lengthy
And the energy and preserve it would need to come up to the surface…

Such is the energy required for larger blooming roses
So I thank God I had planted many different variety of flowers
Here in my humble homey garden's oasis

Perhaps each poem….a moment in my life
Small lessons and little happiness in these short vignettes
Giving me a much needed confidence
For that big rush of breath needed to capture a turning moment…
To grasp on tightly to that larger blooming fragrant flower
The queen flower of romance
The flower that will define our love, our life
Our own unique variety of rose

Our Rose…Our Story…

The sweet memories we were able to plant little by little
The sacrifices that we have both endured
Each tear we had withheld

The many homes we've built painstakingly together, brick by brick
The foundation of our life slowly solidifying and slowly cementing

Every step leading to another larger and wider door
The children that we were raising
With their laughter many small roses appeared
Each milestone we were able to celebrate with our family
The love and respect they gave, our happiness grew

We've toiled, nurtured, guided, and cultivated this colorful garden
It is now time to smell those wondrous flowers and roses
Mini or full, the rose that defines our love, our life
Let us both enjoy it now, in this moment when it is in full bloom
Knowing only too well...the finicky of a rose's life.

Morning Rituals…Sipping Coffee

Sometimes…
I am seated under the eave near my large koi pond
Abundant with dozens of paired koi
Mesmerizing me each morning to see them swimming in tandem
Their unique spots and colors-males and females- yin and yang
As they crowd each other for their own morning rituals
    of simple fish pellets
Sharing their spaces with the morning or evening's water lilies
And fragrant lotus -short-lived beautiful flowers-
    sprinkled throughout the pond
Where dragonflies, butterflies and an assortment of birds
    that come unexpectedly by to visit

Sometimes…
I am enjoying a cup set amidst the picturesque Koolau mountain
Beautiful peaceful Kaneohe bay along the shore of Waikane
The vast ocean and mirrored reflections of the calming waters
With the Chinaman Moks in full display
I would sit inside the hammock between the two bent coconut trees
Hidden amongst the mangroves, making for a private retreat
Sharing my solitude with the passing geckos
Feeling in awe to see that there is life underneath the calm sea
When a fish jumps out of the water unexpectedly

Sometimes…
I am sitting on a bench alone under the pergola of my own design
Looking in awe toward the majestic Koolau mountains' silhouette

Where multitudes of waterfalls cascade down along its ridges
When the rain has fallen deep into the mountain,
    and the mist hovers ever so magically
The fresh smell and greenery of the windward side
    always revives an artist's soul

Sometimes...
Overlooking the bay facing the eastern seas toward Portlock
Watching serenely for the soft gradual light, the nascent of day
Washing the sky with water-colored pink dreams
In tune with the morning larks chirping merrily
Greeting the hopeful day with sweet fragrances
Comingling with the smell of heavenly bliss
    from the nocturnal passing
Driving down the slope of Hawaii Loa Ridge
    and rising above Koko Head mound
The sun washing the sky in intense cadmium red splendor
The vividness of the sun blazing in tandem with the departing moon,
    still present above Diamond Head Crater
I feel blessed to be able to see both Sun and Moon in the same sky

Sometimes...
Gazing at the busy street of a newly found city or country
    I happened to visit
Sitting quietly in a secluded place in a far away hotel
The many places, and spaces that I have borrowed
All for the simple act of enjoying my morning cup of elixir

Reflecting...

Today it's under the large spacious porch of my newly built home
Yesterday it was under the pergola of a home against the Koolaus
Before it was facing the bay in the small cove near Makaha

Be it alone on the porch in the dew of morning
Or in a small café in another town or country
The day always starts anew wherever I may be
The day brings hope and appreciation for whatever may unfold

I greet each and every morning with a soft smile
And quietly thank God for all his amazing grace
As I sip my cup of aromatic coffee....enjoying my morning ritual.

Early Morning and Evening Symphony

Awaking to the sounds of the morning larks chirping
Feeling the freshness of a brand new day
Enjoying the gentle breeze that fills the senses
Playing in duet to the sky awash in gentle pink foray
The morning ritual thus begins

Freshly brewed convenient coffee pods in place
Soon the aroma of Starbuck permeates my nostrils
Happily I take my cup of morning elixir
Sitting contently on the large open veranda
Sipping, thinking, reflecting, and enjoying each sight and sound
The large banyan tree's canopy spread in front of my neighbor's house
Each day, an appreciation of nature's momentous gifts and spirits
Each day the early morning symphony begins…

Today,
Early morning kisses and embrace
He drips my morning cup of elixir unhurried
He drives me to work with sweetness on his face
He gives me loving messages throughout the day
He picks me up and waits patiently for a chance
Holding hands, touching gently, looking sweetly into my eyes
Until our evening rituals slowly thus begins

He makes me dinner with love and tender care
We partake of our meals in gentle spirits
Kissing and embracing and holding until it's time

Strolling under the evening sky hand in hand
Or often times with our newly found companion
Our furry four-legged friend
As we share this path of our life now in unison
Under the stars and the many phases of the bright moon above

It is hard to believe we've known each other for decades
Seeing both of us now so inseparable
We are looking at each other for the first time
Not as a father and a mother, not of being a daughter or a son

We are sharing now our individual dreams that we had given up
We are sharing now the pride we were forced to leave behind
We are strolling gently into that new horizon, into that new dimension
Until it is time for our nightly rituals, full of anticipation
As husband and as his wife
Thus our evening symphony begins…

He said he would give his life for me
He tells me to live a great life
His love holds the key to my great life.

Heart's Reflection

The love for our children equals the love for our parents
The sacrifices for our children reflect the sacrifices
Our parents gave us
The heart's mirror reflects what it sees.

Balance of the Four Seasons

When *"Spring" Fall*s too early
Flowers do not have enough time to
Strengthen and insulate their roots

When *"Winter"* comes on too strong
"Summer" days will thus be shortened.

The Webs of Our Life

In the webs of our life
You will meet monsters and predators, disguised as
    admirers and flatterers
You will meet destroyers of dreams, and silencers of your poetry
You will meet adversaries and weaklings, relishing in your every fall

In the webs of your life
You will meet kindness amongst strangers who cross your path
You will feel the *Butterfly Effects* of all the sacrifices
    you have had to make
And the generous gifts of smiles you gave along the way

In the webs of your life
You may never know why the *Shooting Stars* are there to guide you
But needed to trust in the messages they gave
You will meet your *White Knight*
Whose self-righteousness is, at times, suffocating
But for whom you will be the ultimate test

In the webs of your life
As husband and wife, will you need to merge in like-mind?
Or be two individuals, each with their own independent dreams
In loving your husband, do you give up yourself?
In loving his wife, will he be able to celebrate with her
The formidable woman that she has become

Or does he long to protect that insecure little girl
Who she was forced to leave far, far behind

Because it was all in *God's Arrangements* after all
That we are who we have become
By crossing paths with these people
In The Webs of Our Life!

Woman in Veil

Quiet, tender, and guarded
A young woman in veil
Mysterious, feminine, and reflective
A poised woman in veil
Percipient, contemplative, and protective
As she cautiously...unveils.

A Silhouette in Time

A young girl
With hair, silk-draped divine
Flowing, swaying
In the evening's gentle breeze

A feminine form
Slender and timeless, forever
Strolling, reflecting
Under the starlit sky

A mysterious woman
Often misunderstood
Quietly smiling
Contemplative and resigned

A softened soul
Embracing life, and her sojourn
Gently opening
The windows to her mind.

Fool or Wise

A fool only wants to fall in love
A wise man wants to stay in love

A fool only knows how to fall in love
A wise man knows how to keep his love

Fool or wise
A woman only wants to be loved.

Epilogue

"...In Reaching the Shore"

"I view life as a wave coming to shore. Before it finds or reaches its shore, it must go through many different phases. At the beginning, the wave is unpredictable. It goes through many ups and downs. Gradually though, its peaks are not as high but more subtle, until it finally reaches its shore. In reaching its shore, it has found peace and tranquility."

I had penned those words in my senior year of high school and had later recited those same words in a speech for the Miss Chinatown Pageant. I have seen numerous ups and downs since then.

In all of our lives we will each ride our own sets of waves. No one is above perfection, no one is invincible, and no one can ride those waves to shore alone.

In my own vessel, I have gone through many turbulent waves, but finally the tranquil shore was seen up ahead. As I reached the shore, a gallant gentleman stood waiting. He stretched out his hand offering to help. I willingly and happily grasped on tightly as he pulled me up to stand beside him on firmer ground. With his other hand he offered me a much-needed nourishment. Graciously I accepted the ice-cream cone, as I gave him a laughing smile. This time his name and face would be deeply ingrained within me, as he is the beacon that has been my constant guide through the ever-changing mist. I held lovingly the ice cream cone that my dear husband gave, and thanked God that I had made it safely to our shore.

A Poet's Final Note...
The Poetic Mind...

Poets are naturally introspective by nature. We live in our minds, and hold our thoughts deeply and dearly, close to us. Most people would even say we are emotionless at time, as we are immensely private. We are that wallpaper or dragonfly, observing and hovering quietly above our surrounding, and then will rearrange the world romantically and artistically in our mind. We are both dreamer and idealist; wanting to feel all emotions, yet at times, we may hold at bay that "sweet surrender" when we sustain our emotions from following through. We will resist "living it out", so we then must "write it down."

Though perhaps not true for all poets, but for myself, my writing and speaking persona may be contradicting. Perhaps those formative years had played a tremendous impact on my life, and had rendered me speechless in certain aspects. So when speech evades me, my other senses are thus heightened.

As a poet, I may find great beauty in a person's intimate moment of hesitation, in letting things go unsaid, in bringing a reader to that moment of a pause on that "knock" on the door, upon reflection, stop mid way only to then walk away... My artistic thoughts and mind will make up differing scenarios and differing endings. I may find beauty in the exquisite pain of always keeping the "hunger", of always keeping the "yearning" alive, and oftentimes always resisting giving into the temptations, which are all a part of human nature.

In this, perhaps my life is as it is. My husband has always kept me "hungry" and "yearning"-for he is the Sun-transfix, and I am the many phases of the evolving and revolving Moon. His light is always shining, always encompassing, while I move from lightness to darkness, sometime closer to him, sometime further away. My light shines brightest in the calm of the night when it is full, and while most may be in slumber. My beauty will be revealed and appreciated only when the heart needs to navigate its way home.

Often, briefly we are in the same sky- Sun and Moon- looking across at each other. But for most of the time, one must always *Rise then Set* in order to let the other *Set then Rise*. This is the exquisite pain of loving him. I hope that I have paid him an honor in these poems. Such is a Man for whom a Woman will stand tall against all tempters abound...As I tell him definitively now, how much I love him, and that to behold and hold onto dearly as the Sun and the Moon have now eclipses.

Acknowledgements

Being an introvert, it would take most people more than half a decade of interactions before they would come to know my name. Being shy in an interactive industry is a contradiction naturally. Most would only know my smile and perhaps in their misunderstanding of my personality, taking timidity for aloofness, they kept their distance or they just simply labeled me as the salesperson that I am.

It would take some convincing at the beginning to tell them that I am indeed the Proprietor. Therefore, this is an acknowledgment to those individuals who intuitively saw the deeper side of who I am without my telling them. Without their respect and silent admiration-**the fuel I need**- it would have been hard even for the purest of **INTJ*or INFJ*** personality to thrive. Both personalities are very rare.

R. Luerson, my first boss and an MIT graduate, who had initially insulted me, would give me the greatest boost of my very short career in architecture. His action, of increasing my salary by 60% after working the summer, thereby making the entire office stop by my desk to see my work, would give me my first breath of self-confidence.

T. Allen, a friend and realtor who is a Top Producer in her own career, also commented to me…"*It's obvious you are good at what you are doing…*"

G. and R. Shimabukuro, upon his terminal diagnosis, asked his wife to bring him to my store in order to say farewell. That remains the highest honor that I have experienced in my own career. There would be many more similar situations later.

The many patrons who became friends, their *strength in numbers*, gave me much confidence to *rise and stand amongst the many few*. They are truly the inspiration and relationship accruements that have kept me going in my long professional tenure. I am blessed and honored to be able to share with them some of the joyous and significant moments in their lives.

Dr. Lien, a cardiologist and Tracy, his incredible and beautiful wife, generously extended courtesy and respect towards my family and me.

In Tracy, I found a kindred spirit, as we both have our own crosses to bear. Tracy along with my daughter Isabella, are my two cheerleaders.

Isabella is my best friend, confidant, co-editor, and also my beautiful and intelligent daughter. She and her two brothers are the glue that binds our family.

My two sons: Alan and Andre. They are the Joys, the Loves, and the Sunshine In My Life. The children, along with our new puppy Ace have kept my life light-hearted and sweet!

The Chinese Chamber of Commerce and the Miss Chinatown Hawaii Committee, for honoring me with the title of Miss Chinatown Hawaii 1989. This title was one of the highlights of my life.

Dr. Lawrence, who is my guardian angel and Dr. Stice, a former Miss Hawaii, who years ago generously gave up her time and talent to teach me my dance routine for the pageant. I could never grasp that "seductive" move, then and now, and was happy to leave it out of the routine! They are the epitome of talent, intelligence and kindness.

M.M.Kaye, the author of *The Far Pavilion* and *Shadow of the Moon*, was my idol. Both novels are set in India. It is hard to believe, as only an introvert would emphatically state, that the latter book, "Shadow of the Moon..." has been a constant companion, ergo a best friend to me, in the four decades after my coming upon it by chance. Kaye's writing style in certain scenarios is full of subtlety and innuendo. Her writing allows the readers to envision and complete her crucial words in their own minds, thus leaving the readers still partially craving... yet happily satiated.

I thank my friends, Tram, Victoria, Nga, Dora, Trang-my sister-in-law, and my sisters Olivia and Jeannie, for their listening ears during my darkest moments. Dora and Tram are also the few people with whom I could discuss philosophical ideology and spirituality. I am grateful for their friendships and encouragements in my writing project. Dora and Tram are also the few people with whom I am able to share my writings.

My entire family for being in my life: Spearheaded by my beautiful mom, Carol Wu, and the guiding-light, Michael Wu, my father.

My siblings: Tan, Trung, Hoa, Viet, Nam, Hung, Cuong, Lien, *Minh* (as Thanh Minh is my given name), Hiep, Hoi, Huu, Hoa.

To Kathryn Takara, my editor and publisher. I had always dreamt of being discovered and mentored by another woman. The vision had always occurred on the beach where I am always alone contemplating. Without meeting her, I could never have fulfilled the last wish on my bucket list.

Most Importantly, I thank my dear husband, Hoang, who with his extremely rare compliment said, "Lily, you deserve this!" upon the completion of the house I had designed and that he had built for me on the picturesque tranquil waters in Waikane. His compliments were very sparse, but greatly needed and appreciated. I also thank him for being the *Polaris** in our life and in raising and caring for our beautiful three children.

Perhaps we are too much alike in many endeavors and that we are in each other's blind spot that the elements of *Fire and Water* are thus heightened and magnified. Or that nothing is ever too perfect in life. I also thank him deeply for loving all the chapters in my life, the *Winters and Summers*, the *Fire and Water*, and especially the *Springs and Falls* of our lives together. Thankfully, we are able to enjoy and treasure the latest chapter, *Of Husband...And of His Wife*, together at last...

Lastly, I want to thank God for His grace and many gifts. I have experienced the deepest physical and emotional pains in life- from north to south and from front to back-but I would also know the greatest joys of both mind and body; the internal and external karma has aligned. God reveals to me things that I am meant to see, feel, and hear, when I am ready and wise enough to receive and appreciate them. For a poet, the plethora of emotions and experiences are the greatest gifts. In this life I am well blessed, well loved, and well respected, and my wishes have been realized. Thank you, God, for I am deeply humbled by your gifts and by your many arrangements in my life.

From the Myers-Briggs 16 Personality Types:
**INTJ: Introverted, Intuitive, Thinking, Judging (the Female Architect)*
**INFJ: Introverted, Intuitive, Feeling, Judging (the Poet)*
**Polaris-Another name for the North Star that remains constant in the night sky.*

Photo Credit: Taylor Pham Circa 2019

About the Author

Lily is a Libra, born in the year of the Fire Sheep. She has called Hawaii home for the past 45 years and lives with her husband and three children. She is a respected businesswoman. She has designed, built and renovated her many businesses and residences.

Lily received a Bachelor of Architecture Degree from UH Manoa. She is a former Miss Chinatown Hawaii 1989, as well as Miss Congeniality. She is a former cheerleader and National Honor Society member. Lily has won scholarships to the Hawaii Academy of Art, Honorable Mentions in science fair competition, as well as various awards and accolades.

Lily is presently happy running her single location storefront, in which she has worked since her first year of college. She also enjoys keeping a somewhat Zen environment, singing karaoke (even if it's out of tune), staring at the moon and stars, taking long strolls, experimenting in the kitchen, and doing various art projects. She is currently exploring gardening, as well as spending time reflecting, as she also enjoys doing absolutely nothing at all. This is her first completed writing project.

www.ingramcontent.com/pod-product-compliance
Lightning Source LLC
Chambersburg PA
CBHW051548010526
44118CB00022B/2628